THIS OR THAT? History

Living in the
JAMESTOWN
COLONY

A This or That Debate

by Jessica Rusick

CAPSTONE PRESS
a capstone imprint

Capstone Captivate is published by Capstone Press, an imprint of Capstone.
1710 Roe Crest Drive
North Mankato, Minnesota 56003
www.capstonepub.com

Library of Congress Cataloging-in-Publication Data is available on the Library of Congress website.
ISBN: 978-1-4966-8387-8 (library binding)
ISBN: 978-1-4966-8785-2 (paperback)
ISBN: 978-1-4966-8438-7 (eBook PDF)

Summary: The Jamestown colony was established in 1607 as the first permanent English settlement in North America. Test your decision-making skills with this or that questions related to living there!

Image Credits
Alamy: Gado Images, 26, Mark Summerfield, 27; ClipArt ETC: Edward S Ellis, Ellis's History of the United States, 6; Flickr: Internet Archive Book Images, 24; iStockphoto: powerofforever, 23; Library of Congress: Jan Jansson, 32, Cover (map); Shutterstock Images: ananaline, 30, Erni, 17, eurobanks, Cover (corn), Fotos593, 21, Gula52, 13, IgorXII, 18, Joe Farah, 16, Junjira Limcharoen, 12, Kathy Clark, 8, Krasula, 28, MICHAEL D. BURKHALTER, Cover (blacksmith shop), Steve Heap, Cover (fort), Tyniansky Yury, 19, Zoran Milic, 5; U.S. National Park Service: John Heinly, 7, Sidney E. King, artist, 3, 4–5, 9, 10, 11, 14, 15, 20, 22, 25; Wikimedia Commons: Wellcome Library, London, 29

Design Elements: Jan Jansson/Library of Congress (background map)

Editorial Credits
Editor: Rebecca Felix; Designers: Aruna Rangarajan & Tamara JM Peterson; Production Specialist: Tori Abraham

All internet sites appearing in back matter were available and accurate when this book was sent to press.

A ROUGH START

In May 1607, 104 men arrived in modern-day Virginia to establish the Jamestown colony. A group of Englishmen called the Virginia Company paid for this undertaking. The group hoped colonists would find valuables such as gold in the New World and send it back to England.

The colonists faced many challenges. They did not have good water to drink or good weather to grow food. Many got sick. Some starved. By 1608, only 38 were still alive.

By 1613, the colonists were growing **tobacco**. They shipped it to England to be sold. These sales helped Jamestown become successful. It became the first permanent English colony in America.

HOW TO USE THIS BOOK

What if you had been a colonist in Jamestown? What choices would you have made along the way? Do you think you would have survived?

This book is full of questions that relate to life in Jamestown. Some of them are questions real people had to face. The questions are followed by details to help you come to a decision.

THE JAMESTOWN COLONY

KEY
Location

N
W ⊙ E
S

Jamestown
(in present-day
Virginia)

Pick one choice or the other. There are no wrong answers! But just like the colonists, you should think carefully about your decisions.

Are you ready? Turn the page to pick this or that!

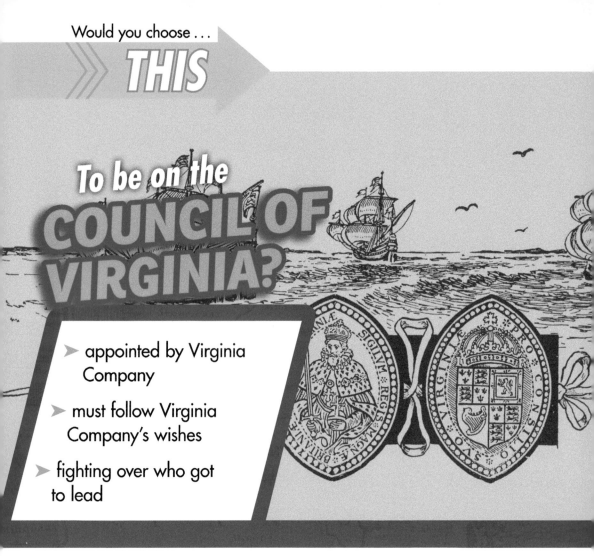

THIS

To be on the
COUNCIL OF VIRGINIA?

➤ appointed by Virginia Company

➤ must follow Virginia Company's wishes

➤ fighting over who got to lead

The Virginia Company chose the people who were in the first government of Jamestown. Its members had to do what the Virginia Company wanted. Colonists learned who would be on the council after arriving in Jamestown. Some people grew unhappy with the leaders' abilities and decisions. This led to fighting among the colonists.

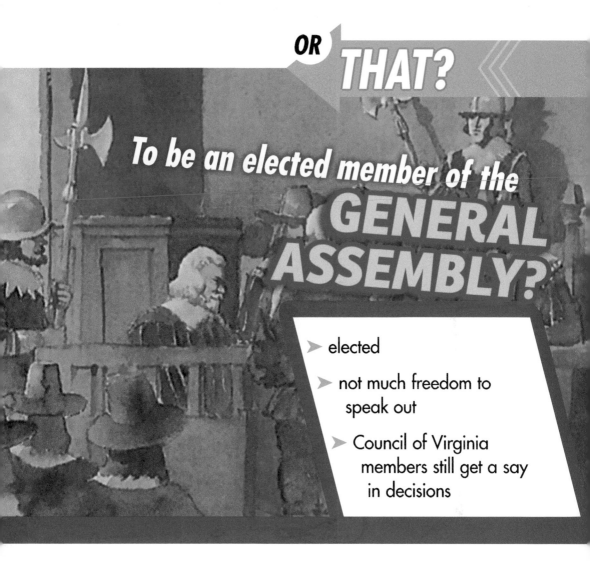

To be an elected member of the **GENERAL ASSEMBLY?**

➤ elected

➤ not much freedom to speak out

➤ Council of Virginia members still get a say in decisions

The General Assembly governed Jamestown starting in 1619. Colonists elected some of its members. But the Council of Virginia still existed as part of the Assembly. Council members sat in on all meetings and had the power to influence decisions. So General Assembly members did not have total freedom to rule.

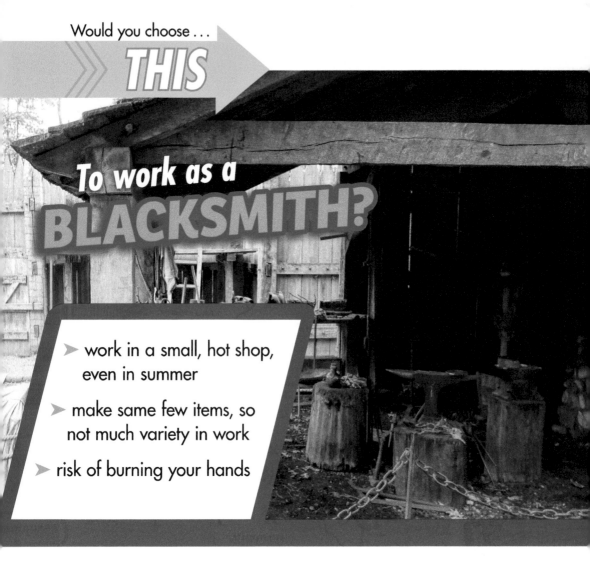

THIS

To work as a

BLACKSMITH?

- ➤ work in a small, hot shop, even in summer
- ➤ make same few items, so not much variety in work
- ➤ risk of burning your hands

Jamestown's blacksmiths made and repaired tools. They heated metal bars over coal fires. Then they shaped the metal into different items. Blacksmiths worked in small, dark shops. The coal fires made the shops very hot. Blacksmiths' faces and clothing were covered with **soot**. They risked burning their hands in the fire.

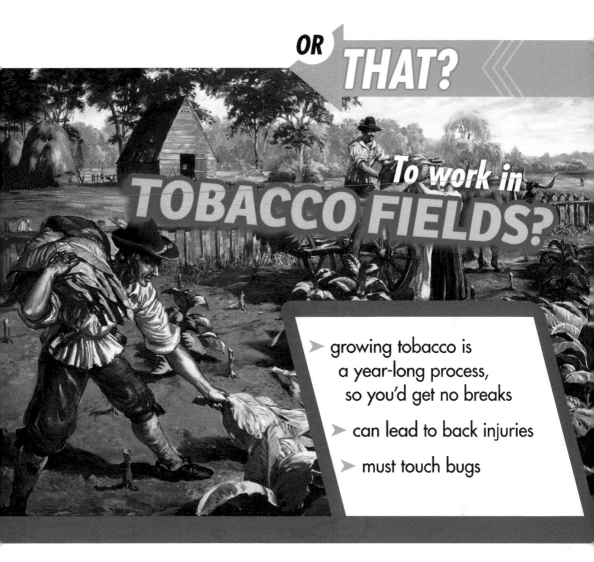

To work in
TOBACCO FIELDS?

➤ growing tobacco is
   a year-long process,
   so you'd get no breaks

➤ can lead to back injuries

➤ must touch bugs

Growing tobacco was a long process. It required
many steps done by hand. One step was to build
hundreds of small dirt hills for seedlings. This made
a worker's hands and clothes dirty. Once the tobacco
grew taller, workers had to pick tobacco worms off
the leaves one by one.

Would you choose . . .

THIS

To farm SILKWORMS?

➤ long process with many steps

➤ involves working with bugs all day, including boiling them

➤ high chance of failure

Colonists tried to make many products to send to England. One was **silk**. Silk comes from the cocoons of bugs called silkworms. To get the silk, colonists roasted and boiled the cocoons. Silkworms eat leaves. But they did not prefer the leaves that grew in Jamestown. The worms produced poor-quality silk or no silk at all. Eventually, Jamestown's silk industry failed.

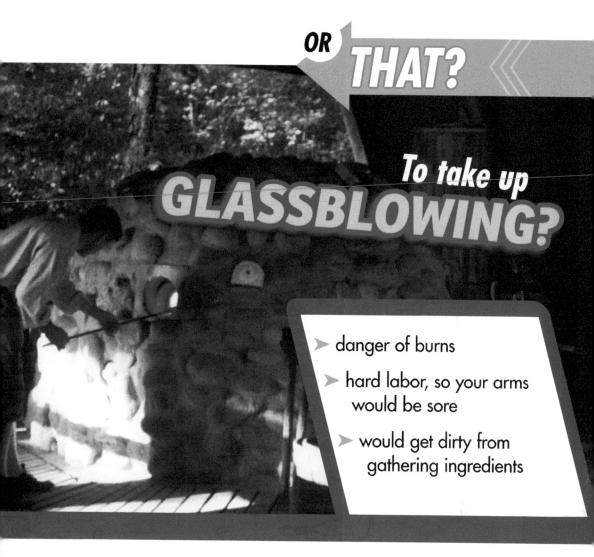

To take up
GLASSBLOWING?

➤ danger of burns

➤ hard labor, so your arms
would be sore

➤ would get dirty from
gathering ingredients

Glassblowers made bottles and vases. They worked over fires to heat and shape glass. These fires were about 2,200 degrees Fahrenheit (1,200 degrees Celsius)! A glassblower spent a lot of time gathering firewood. He also had to gather glass ingredients. This included heavy sand, slimy seaweed, and oyster shells.

Would you choose . . .

THIS

To

DIG FOR GOLD ORE?

- dirty, tiring work
- could get tricked by fool's gold
- likely would not find much

The Virginia Company wanted colonists to look for gold. Some colonists spent days digging in the dirt with pickaxes and shovels. They also dug in muddy riverbanks and squishy bogs. They didn't find much. And what they did unearth was often **fool's gold**. In addition, digging for gold took time away from building the colony.

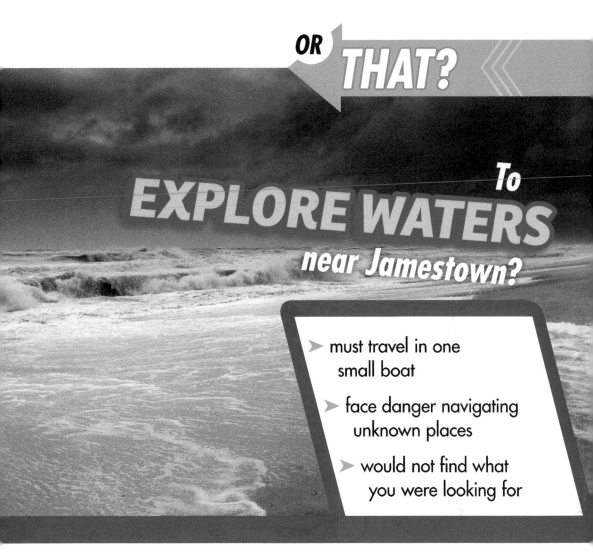

To EXPLORE WATERS near Jamestown?

➤ must travel in one small boat

➤ face danger navigating unknown places

➤ would not find what you were looking for

From 1607 to 1609, groups of colonists explored the James River and Chesapeake Bay. They were looking for a path to the Pacific Ocean. The men traveled in one boat. Depending on how many men were along, the small boat became crowded and uncomfortable. Strong storms on some journeys almost made the boat sink. The men did not find the path they were looking for.

Would you choose . . .

THIS

To get sick with
DYSENTERY?

- caused by drinking dirty water
- brings on dehydration from vomiting and diarrhea
- can kill quickly

Jamestown was built on swampy land. The water was salty and not good to drink. It also grew **polluted** by the colonists' trash and poop. Drinking this water could cause dysentery. This disease causes **vomiting** and **diarrhea**, which leads to a lack of water in the body. This dehydration, paired with bacteria from the dysentery, could kill colonists quickly.

To get sick with
SCURVY?

➤ from eating poorly

➤ causes weakness and bleeding gums

➤ can cause death, especially with other conditions

The colonists landed at Jamestown during a **drought**. Lack of rain made it hard for them to grow fruits and vegetables. Without vitamin C from these foods, many colonists suffered scurvy. This disease made them weak. Scurvy also caused bruises, bleeding gums, and rotting teeth. Scurvy could be deadly if left untreated, especially if colonists were also sick with other illnesses.

Would you choose . . .

THIS

To
EAT A SNAKE
during the "starving time"?

➤ could choke on small bones

➤ danger of eating venom

➤ meat can be hard to chew

The winter of 1609 was known as the "starving time." Because of a drought, colonists were not able to grow enough food to store for winter. Some caught and ate snakes to survive. Certain snakes were **venomous**. These could be dangerous to eat. If the venom got into a colonist's bloodstream, it would be painful.

To **EAT A RAT** during the "starving time"?

> rats can carry disease

> must skin the rat

> meat has a bad smell

Colonists also ate rats to keep from starving in the winter of 1609. Some rats carry diseases. These diseases could cause fever and diarrhea in people who ate the affected rats. If the rats weren't cooked properly, they could make colonists sick. Rats' bodies also produce a stinky oil. Even after rats are cooked, this oil can make them smell like pee!

To help
DIG A WELL?

> dirty work digging in mud
> could get back injuries
> could fall in well

Colonists dug a well to get fresh drinking water from underground. The well was 14 feet (4 m) deep. This meant lots of digging in the dirt and mud. The repeated motion of digging could cause back injuries. Colonists likely also had to lift heavy buckets of dirt from the well. Workers were also in danger of falling into the well or getting buried in dirt during a cave-in.

To help
CUT DOWN TREES?

➤ risk of having tree fall on you

➤ risk of shoulder injury

➤ danger of cutting yourself with an ax

Colonists cut down trees to clear land and get wood to build their fort. Thirty laborers worked to cut down between 500 and 600 trees. Swinging an ax repeatedly could cause shoulder injuries. Cutting trees could be dangerous in other ways too. The workers were at risk of cutting themselves with their axes. They could also be injured if a falling tree hit them.

Would you choose . . .

THIS

To be an apprentice to an

APOTHECARY?

➤ must be around sick people

➤ would spend lots of time outside, possibly in bad weather

➤ encounter dangerous plants

Apothecaries tried to cure people's illnesses. They spent a lot of time around sick people. They made medicines out of plants and herbs. This was often dirty work. Many plants in the New World were unfamiliar to colonists. Apothecaries did not know which ones were dangerous to touch or use.

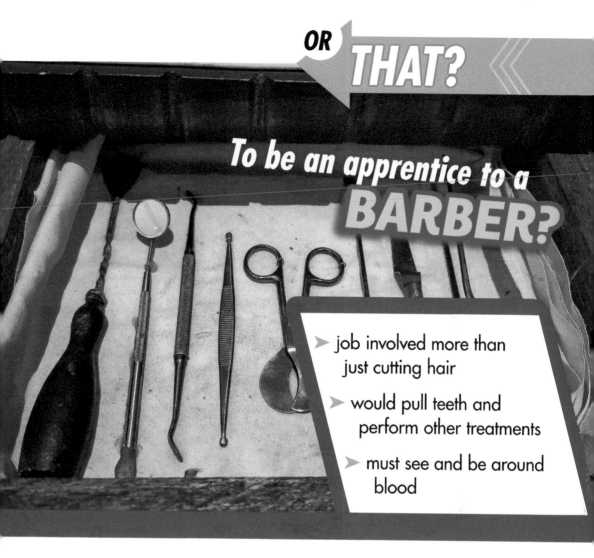

To be an apprentice to a
BARBER?

➤ job involved more than
  just cutting hair

➤ would pull teeth and
  perform other treatments

➤ must see and be around
  blood

Just like today, barbers in Jamestown trimmed hair
and beards. But they also did small surgeries. They
pulled rotting teeth. They also likely removed **boils**
and other growths from people's bodies. In some cases,
barbers may even have had to perform **bloodletting**.

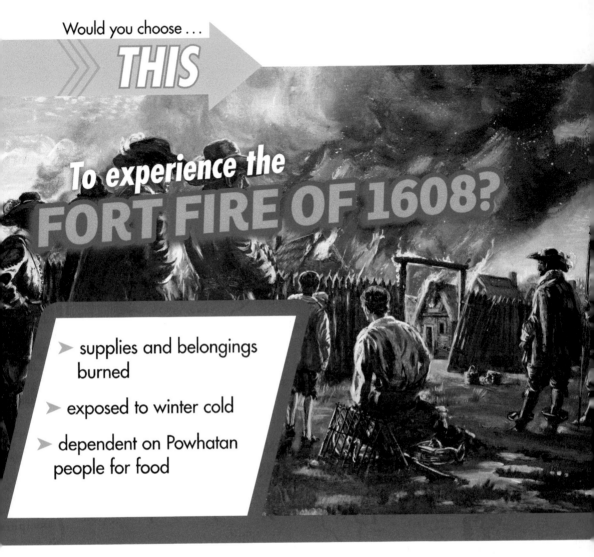

Would you choose . . .

THIS

To experience the
FORT FIRE OF 1608?

- supplies and belongings burned
- exposed to winter cold
- dependent on Powhatan people for food

Many colonists lived in buildings that made up Fort James. In January 1608, a fire destroyed the fort. People lost their homes and belongings. The fire also ruined supplies and food. Colonists had to rebuild shelters in the freezing cold. They became even more dependent on the Powhatans for food.

To experience the
SHIPWRECK OF 1609?

➤ supplies and belongings ruined by water

➤ forage for food to survive

➤ stuck on an island for months

In 1609, a ship bringing new colonists and supplies to Jamestown shipwrecked in Bermuda. Passengers tossed many supplies overboard to lighten the ship and keep it afloat. On the island, colonists ate sea turtles, wild pigs, and more to survive. After nine or 10 months, they built two boats from the ship's wreckage. They then sailed to Jamestown.

Would you choose...

THIS

To live under

EDWARD MARIA WINGFIELD?

> ➤ colonists went hungry under his leadership

> ➤ Wingfield was accused of hogging food

> ➤ removed from his position by colonists

Edward Maria Wingfield was Jamestown's first Council President. He created rules about how much food colonists could eat. Wingfield was accused of starving the colony. He was also accused of keeping the best food for himself. Wingfield was eventually arrested by the colonists. They held a trial and removed him from office.

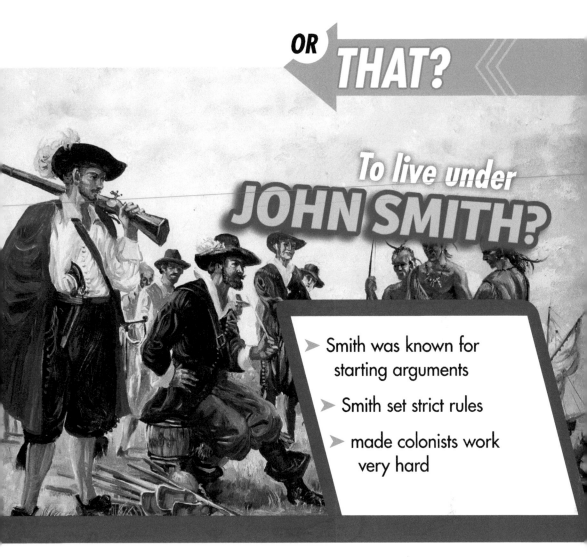

OR THAT?

To live under JOHN SMITH?

- Smith was known for starting arguments
- Smith set strict rules
- made colonists work very hard

John Smith became Council President in 1608. His rules may have helped Jamestown survive. But many colonists thought they were too strict. Smith said colonists who didn't work didn't get to eat. Before that, all colonists got to eat no matter what. Smith made colonists work long days planting crops, digging wells, and fixing buildings.

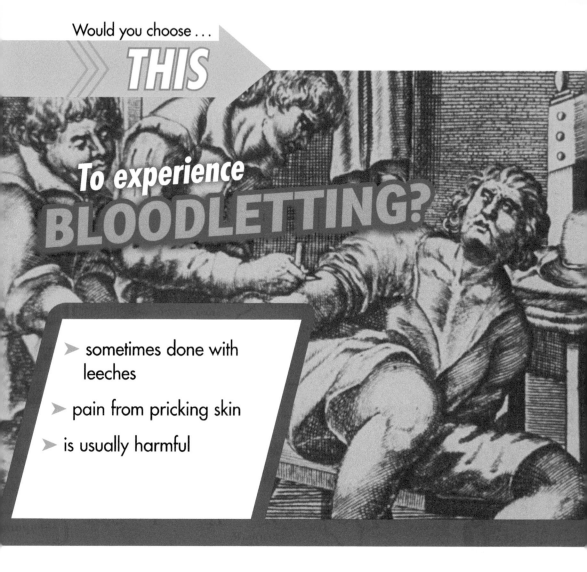

THIS

To experience
BLOODLETTING?

- sometimes done with leeches
- pain from pricking skin
- is usually harmful

Early doctors thought human bodies held four fluids, or **humors**. Blood was one. Doctors thought people got sick when they had too much of any humor. They made patients bleed to "balance the humors." Today, we know this is dangerous. Blood loss causes weakness and can lead to death. It does not work to treat most illnesses.

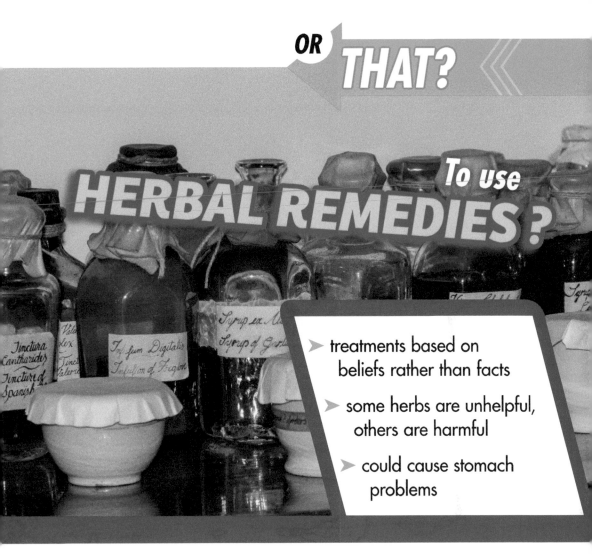

To use

HERBAL REMEDIES?

> treatments based on beliefs rather than facts

> some herbs are unhelpful, others are harmful

> could cause stomach problems

Many colonial doctors thought herbs looked similar to illnesses they treated. For example, forget-me-not flower seed pods look like scorpion tails. So doctors thought the flower cured scorpion bites. But certain herbs doctors used actually caused harm. Jalap was one. If used incorrectly, it caused vomiting and diarrhea.

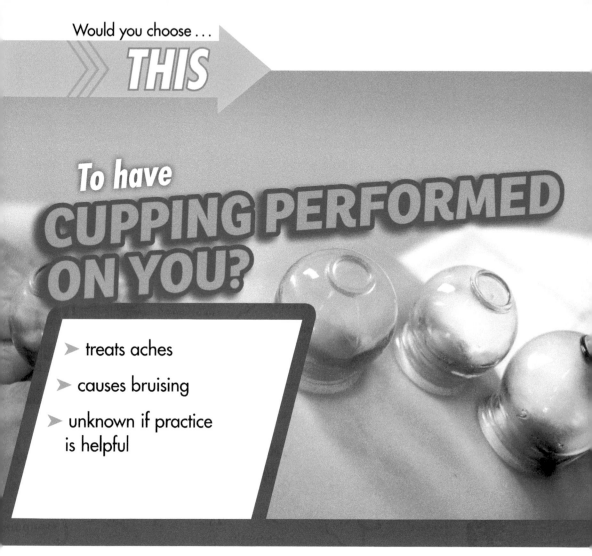

To have
CUPPING PERFORMED
ON YOU?

> treats aches

> causes bruising

> unknown if practice is helpful

Jamestown doctors used cupping to increase a patient's blood flow. This treated aches and numbness. First, a physician heated a glass cup over fire. Then he put the rim of the cup on a patient's bare skin. Cupping left patients with large, circular bruises. Some people still use cupping today. But scientists disagree whether it works as a medical treatment.

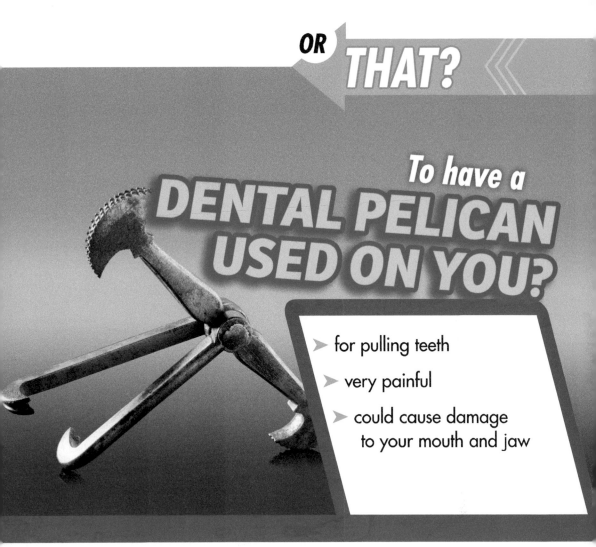

To have a
DENTAL PELICAN
USED ON YOU?

> for pulling teeth

> very painful

> could cause damage
to your mouth and jaw

Jamestown barbers used a dental pelican to pull
teeth. One end was a claw. This was placed over the
tooth. The other end rested on the gums. Barbers
used the pelican to twist people's teeth out of their
mouths. This process could cause gum damage or
harm other teeth.

LIGHTNING ROUND

Would you choose to . . .

➤ be itchy with mosquito bites or head lice?

➤ help tend chickens or help catch fish?

➤ take your favorite book or favorite toy along to Jamestown?

➤ play with an iron toy horse or a toy windmill?

➤ jump rope or practice yo-yo to pass time in the fort?

➤ have cockroaches in your stored clothes or bedbugs in your bed?

➤ make clothes as a tailor or build houses as a carpenter?

➤ trade wool blankets or metal tools with American Indian tribes in exchange for corn?

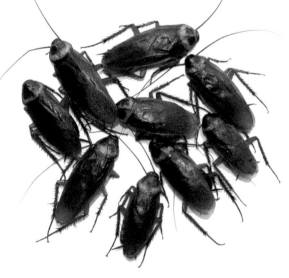

GLOSSARY

bloodletting (BLUHD-leht-ing)—surgical removal of a patient's blood as a medical treatment

boil (BOIL)—a painful swelling on or under the skin

diarrhea (dye-uh-REE-uh)—a condition in which normally solid waste from your body becomes liquid

drought (DROUT)—a long period without rain

fool's gold (FOOLZ GOLD)—a variety of minerals resembling gold

humor (HYOO-mur)—in medieval medicine, one of four fluids of the body that, based on proportions, determined a person's health

polluted (puh-LOOT-ed)—contaminated or made dirty or impure, especially with waste

silk (SILK)—a soft, shiny fiber or thread made by silkworms

soot (SUT)—black powder produced when coal or wood is burned

tobacco (tuh-BAK-oh)—chopped, dried leaves of the tobacco plant, which people use for smoking or chewing

venomous (VEN-uhm-us)—producing a poison called venom

vomit (VAH-mit)—to bring up food from the stomach and expel it through the mouth

READ MORE

Ditchfield, Christin. *Exploring the Virginia Colony*. North Mankato, MN: Capstone Press, a Capstone imprint, 2017.

McAneney, Caitie. *Uncovering the Jamestown Colony*. New York: Gareth Stevens Publishing, 2017.

Omoth, Tyler. *Establishing the American Colonies*. Lake Elmo, MN: Focus Readers, 2018.

INTERNET SITES

Ducksters—Colonial America: Jamestown Settlement
https://www.ducksters.com/history/colonial_america/jamestown_settlement.php

Historic Jamestowne—Jamestown Rediscovery
https://historicjamestowne.org/

National Geographic Kids—On the Trail of Captain John Smith
https://kids.nationalgeographic.com/games/action-and-adventure/on-the-trail-of-captain-john-smith/